Affordable Traffic Solutions

By
Lukwago Juma

Acknowlegement

I want to thank the four people who encouraged me to begin writing this book { Affordable Traffic Solutions }, they where each very important to get this book done. First is my editor, Christopher Brian in USA whom I havenot met physically before, Namasobo Gerald, Ivan Mwesigwa and Robinson. They offered me good comments and criticism on all the content in this book and their responses improved the book immensely.

I particulary want to single out a good friend of mine by the names of Mugisha Fred for his suggestions and comments that where easy to follow and put in place aswell as his incredible turnaround and well comprehensive knowledge of writing.

Finally, I would like to thank createspace for printing and distributing my book through internet retail outlets and other book stores, retails and libraries, therefore I enjoy working with them.

Lukwago Juma.
Kampala, Uganda.
December 2013.

This book is published by createspace a DBA of On-Demand Publishing LLC, part of the Amazon group of companies. Through their services, you can sell books, CDs, and DVDs for a fraction of the cost of traditional manufacturing, while maintaining more control over your materials. They make it simple to distribute your books, music, and video through Internet retail outlets, your own website, and other bookstores, retailers, libraries, and academic institutions

Copyright © 2014 Lukwago Juma

All rights reserved.

ISBN: 10: 149440365X

ISBN-13: 978-1494403652

Contents

Introduction	1
Faze 1	4
Building your Website and a proper website design	4
The role of a website	4
Free traffic Verses Paid Traffic	6
Creating a new website content and ways to create a compelling content when you don't have a clue	7
FAZE 2	11
Search Engine Optimization (SEO)	11
Link –building	16
Free content management system.	16
Blog(S) creation	18
Blog commenting, hopping and Guest hosting	19
Article marketing	20
Press releases	22
FAZE 3	24
Social marketing strategies	24
Viral facebook fan pages	24
About Twitter	30
Linkedin	31
Google +	37
Pinterest	40
Forums	40
FAZE 4	44
Email marketing	44
The difference between email marketing and spam	45

How to create a mailing list	48
Autoresponders	52
Newsletters	53
FAZE 5	56
Creating a Traffic Monster	56
Building Your Traffic Generation Strategy	57
Create the perfect you-tube marketing video and Audio	60
Where to Host Your Content	62
The importance of pictures	65
Social book marking	67
FAZE 6	68
Banner advertisement	68
Pay Per Click (PPC) Advertisement	70
Affiliate programs and Joint venture campaigns	71
Giving away free stuff	74
Mobile and Local free Advertising	75
Take your marketing offline	77
Tips and great ideas	78
Conclusion and a word of encouragement	80
About the author	82

Introduction

Many people always tell you to be patient when it comes to creating your online business. i agree, patience is very important and it has its place, but i believe patience is overrated.

To my view, i think if you want to see your business prosper, why don't you place your foot on the accelerator and see how fast you can reach your goal.

As a matter of fact, you need fuel to get wherever you are going right? and with internet business, your fuel is your website visitor. (Traffic)

The more people you get visiting your website, the faster you're going to reach your online goals and you will have a profitable and a successful online business.

Targeted traffic is integral to your success, this may sound harsh to you, but the fact is if you don't have visitors, you have NO business it's like opening up a grocery and fail to get customers, your business will automatically fail.

There is one thing that I realized very fast when i begun internet business and it was the fact that l needed to drive quite a lot of traffic to my website or blog, i was seriously in need of making money on internet.

When i got started, i tried my hand at PPC (pay per click) traffic eg. facebook and Google Adwords, this caused me a new level of stress where by I was meant to create my campaign and have it approved .l was unable to make profits out of this and i always had to pay over 40 cents per click for a great keyword. So when l realised l was making loses from this paid traffic again.

As you will see, most of my traffic methods don't include google because l may wake up one morning when Google is shut down .Below are the methods that l want to share with you in this book .This is a step by step learning e-course and if you finish up this course , you will definitely generate thousands of visitors to your website without spending a dime. We are going to discuss about the wonderful ideas when it comes to free traffic generation most of the effective methods we are going to cover are free ,you can only pay for traffic If you can only afford it ,you can as well create a budget and a great plan to make it worth your investment .

How would you like to change your life after increasing your income? 20%, 30% or even 50% in the next 2 – 6 months. You're about to learn our proven techniques to drive lots to traffic to your website and blog. We guarantee you will work less and make more, you will then be one of the world's most successful online marketer with a genuine, affordable and high income potential online business that can be operated from your laptop from any where in the world.

We want to make everything perfectly clear before we proceed, this is something more ambitious, deeper and more effective, after getting the targeted traffic that you need, you will definitely be your own boss and write your own paycheck working completely on your own terms from anywhere in the world. Is'nt that wonderful?

Honestly speaking, we are only looking for a limited number of motivated and highly teachable individuals who are willing to learn, unfortunately most people wont put in their time and effort to go through this e-course and set them selves up, perhaps because they are just flatout lazy or simply because they actually don't believe that such a course will be a great benefit for them, remember 90% of these proven methods are free, so endavour to put in your time in order to get setup and understand each and every system. We are here to help you to overcome all the frustrations and obstacles you've always faced when you tried to start or grow your online business, we want you to be the kind of person who will be already making money online and finally finding complete freedom with our step by step proven traffic methods.

Let us move on.

Faze 1

Building your Website and a proper website design

Put it in mind that an effective website attracts customers to your business , it generates sales leads and closes sales as well as multiplying your profits in the process.If you are talented in web design you must combine uniqueness and innovation in design with state of art technology and maintenance support to create a powerful website that produces results.

Nevertheless, you may build it and they don't come ,did you know that some website owners get so disappointed after spending thousands of dollars on their new website(full of different animations, great artwork etc)and no one comes.lts really discouraging and disappointing.

The role of a website

A website is a manually resource and a business tool. Why should you settle for an internet billboard when a website can do so much more? By the way even the smallest business can utilize power of the internet to be more efficient and to build revenue. When you begin thinking about it, you will definitely get excited about the potential of your website.

In other wards, a business website is just one avenue in complete set of business applications that can be used online. Things like, completed surveys, more subscriptions, an increase in average consumer satisfaction, decreased support calls or new sales leads. All of these are measurable goals that do mean something to your company.

What are you really using your website for?The roll of a website and its target audience.Make sure your website adds value in at least one of these four areas below

- Marketing – Generate leads.

- Sales & logistics - Facilitate transactions / order

- Sales ,marketing & help desk – Support

- Human resource ,productions ,accounts public relations - Save money

Think about your target audience and plan (1) how you are going to capture them, (2) what you are going to give them , (3) and how you are going to keep them.

So many online entrepreneurs and affiliates have traffic to their websites but the question is, would you rather have 2000 people visiting your website and don't buy from you? Or have 200 people visiting your website and buy?. Does a good PR (page rank) mean anything to the real profitability of your company? These obstract, relative numbers don't make difference by themselves and should not be the final goal of any website.

Make sure you send your audience the correct and a strong brand message. Actively use your website to build trust, update your website often and communicate with your prospects on twitter or facebook.

The fact is that people are more likely to put trust in your product only if.

-it is consistent and professional if they know more about your product and services they know more about you.

Free traffic Verses Paid Traffic

Of course, this book is all about free traffic generation, but just in case you're second estimate the decision to buy traffic absolute, let's just cover the basics.

Paid definite traffic is about 99% scam. Sure, there is a 1% variable in there somewhere, however statistics show that if you force users to view your website usually through black-handed techniques like URL takeover, malware installations, pop up ads and the works, they are NOT going to be the least bit interested in what you have to offer.

Sadly, this is what most paid traffic sites gives you. You can also take the commercial traffic approach and unsightly advertise your website with local signs collectively, TV/movie commercials, print publications, radio spots or even banner ads on a major search engine. True, you will get guaranteed views…but there is no telling if you will connect with your audience. The best way to market your website is through text related content (or SEO, to

simplify a term), because this means targeted advertising. You only work together with traffic which declare to being interested in your products or services. When you figureout, this is something which requires little or no mental effort. You are directly connecting with your great audience. All that matters now is the presentation.

Creating a new website content and ways to create a compelling content when you don't

have a clue

If you want to be noticed by search engines so as to reach your audience, you have to focus on excellent content. let us leave alone low quantity content and focus on quality content which when you read it it's a reverting language which keeps you interested , it's the type of writing which is always rewarded and beneficial.

A Good content must be:

With good grammer and with proper spelling.

-properly readable

-teaching the audience something good about the subject

-conversation and well entertaining

This infographic is such a phenomenal resource.

Curation:make sure you compile a list of more than 8 favourite blog posts from other blogs.

Group discussions: ask your friends for ideas, consider offline friends, online friends and blogger friends.

Ask your readers: seek for some help from your readers by asking what readers would like to read about or asking a question to get some feedback.

Interview some people: when you write a few questions for some one else to respond to is easier than turning out a whole post.

Allow a guest to write: guests' posts can add content simply to your blog, keep contacting small blogs which could use the publicity and ask them if they would be interested in posting.

Review something: pickup a product or service and write what you like and dislike about it and whether you would recommend it.

Share your success: share with your people step by step how you managed to go to where you are to date. Avoid bragging and share lessons learned along the way.

Share your failures: write about your experience and challenges you faced and what you learned from them.

Pick-up old posts: make sure you remember to pick up some useful old posts and share them with new readers you can also add a description or explanation to each link.

Watch popular movies: when you watch some popular movies, this can be a good place to get ideas.

Television shows: you can choose a TV show which your audience would be likely to watch , look for some of the most popular shows with your target audience.

Top trends: always check google trends to see what's hot right now and work that into your post to boast rankings.

Your personal story: write about your personal story on your blog, this can be a bit hard but it's a great way to connect with your readers.

FAZE 2

Search Engine Optimization (SEO)

Search engine optimization is a methodology of strategies, techniques and tactics used to increase the amount of visitors to a website by obtaining a high ranking placement in the search results pages of a search engine (SERPs) including the big 3 search engines Google, Bing and yahoo as well as other search engines.

SEO helps to ensure that a site is accessible to a search engine and improves the chances that the site will be found by the search engines. It is common practice for internet users to hot click through pages and pages of search results, so where a site ranks in a search is essential for directing more traffic toward the site . the higher a website naturally ranks in organic results of a search , the greater the chance that the site will be visited by the user.

Algorithm: all search engines have something called an algorithm which is the formular that each search engines uses to evaluate web pages and determine their relevance and value when crawling them for possible inclusion in their search engine. A crawler is a robot that browses all of these pages for search engine.

The significance of a genuine keyword strategy

There is one fact I would like to show in this pack ,never

allow the keyword research to affect the standard of your writing ,nevertheless make sure that the keywords you want to focus on when writing never let it affect the standard of the reader ,however the priority here is to write down for human beings but not search engines You not only try hard for quality content but you must focus on a fashionable and nice keyword phrases .After all, no matter what inspired content you come up with if you don't plan together with your keywords ,you will not reach that targeted audience .Bear in mind that targeting your traffic is extremely necessary .in otherwords ,you may also be shopping for mindless ,in visible traffic .you will know right away the kind of user who closes your window before she or he even read the first line.

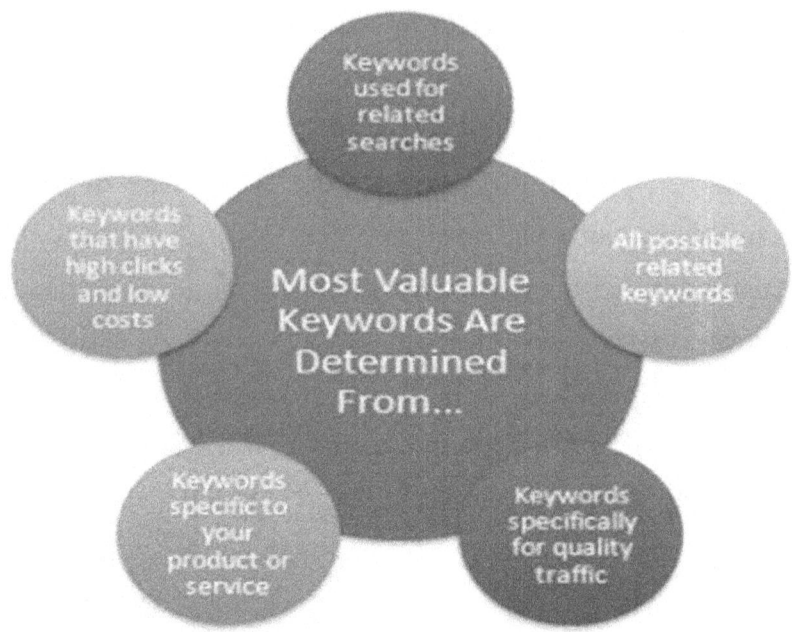

Give time to keyword analysis employing a Google keyword analysis tool or any number of analysis applications .Its good to think about other means of approach .including:

- Keywords for native space traffic

- Niche keywords or long tail key words (long phrases or entire sentences)

- Researching keywords that restrict seamlessly into a sales presentation.

- Wanting up high request keyword.

- Looking up low competition keywords.

- Seeing the chosen keywords of your competitors.

- Estimating what phrases your customers search for.

When you recognize the most prominent or important keywords to your campaign ,you will possibly begin building content then making an attempt to figure in strange keyword phrases in at the instant .search engines place high priority in articles and options that look natural.

However, this is an important issue to recollect when coming up with keyword density .within the past , a high density of 50 or more was acceptable .This controlled outdated algorithms and helped to build website quality in an exceeding short amount of your time. However the most recent role updates penalize sites for the follow of "over optimizing", on the other side implication of low quality writing(or recycled writing)that phrase probably refers to the overuse of keywords.

I deally ,the best quality writing does not actually require keyword density ,quality writing is ruled by the ideal of natural repetition ,exploitation revenant words and statements just for stress .This was a fundamental weakness of the first net world that may solely index pages supported them page titles and high density of revenant keyword phrases.

The new rule updates get to put this issue right and in fact penalize websites that increase keyword repetition .your safest bet is to analise your keywords accurately and target for 125 densities , regardless of the article dictates ,supported intelligent human reading.

Link –building

Link building is the process of establishing relevant inbound links to your website which helps your website to achieve higher rankings with the major search engines and drive target traffic to your website.There are many unethical link building companies out there which employ some pretty shady practices which end up hurting our website instead of helping it.

Free content management system.

Content management system (CMS) is important to your business because it increases efficiency, the content can be pushing easily and efficiency as editing and revision do not require visual design or coding knowledge. The updates will be fast and efficient which will save your business constant time.

Cms will increase your search engine ranking by improving or maintaining your search engine ranking your business has to remain relevant, a good and easy to use cms will help your publishers keep the content fresh.

Cms will help your visitors in their search for information and with a powerful Cms search engine new content is indexed automatically, so it can be found instantly, visitors can also use taxonomy applications, sorting lists, saved searches and move to personalise the search experience.

Cms will save content in a draft state, manage it through folders or taxonomy , easily update site navigation , restrict access auto publishing , style up your content using WYSIWYG editor , Cms can as well help in building websites e.g. Drupal , wordpress and joomla.

Did you know that when you use word press to create your blog or your website can benefit you because it has a huge popularity? Word press is easy to use, it has auto plugins for search engine submissions, you can simply insert META tags by just typing, you can carry out auto integration of your site to your other pages especially social Network pages .

Cms can also improve online branding your marketing team can keep your business relevant by multi channel campaign management eg. Brochures, emails, hyper sites, Rss etc.

Blog(S) creation

Well ,let me define what a blog is: A blog is a website in which items are posted on a usual basis and displaced in reverse chronological order .The term blog is a shortened form of weblog or weblog .Authoring a blog ,maintaining a blog or adding an article to an existing blog is called "blogging" individual articles on a blog are called blog posts, posts or entries .A person who posts these entries is called blogger .A blog comprises text, hyper text, mages and links(to other WebPages and to video, audio and other files).

Blogs use a conversational style of documentation .often blogs focus on a particular "area of interests" such as Washington DC's political goings-on and some blogs discuss personal experiences.

Comments: Not all blogs use comments BUT most do-some blogs are monologue and others are conversational, you can give me a feedback on almost everything I write simply by clicking the comments link at the bottom of each one of the posts this will take you to a little form where you leave your name, email and link to your own blog if you have one as well as your feedback,

comment, Critique, question, essay on why you love my blog promise of money etc).

A great way to learn about blogs is to read a few ,leave some comments ask questions and bookmark your favourites .Learn more about blogs by simply creating your own today ,you can either sign up on: **www.wordpress.com** or **www.blogger.com**, read and follow the instructions on how to create your own blog in a better way.

Blog commenting, hopping and Guest hosting

Did you know that commenting on blog posts is another great way of generating traffic to your website(S) and as well as to begin blogging , you can either use: **www.blogger.com** or **www.wordpress.com**.

Blog hopping is a collection of fans when people get to

discover you, they will remain loyal and may be befriend one another in the process always make it appoint to create valuable content and do everything you can to encourage a community creation.

Not only should you try to follow up on comments, but you should also try to reach out to the blogging community and comment on your visitors' own blogs. If you use a system like Blogger, or even WordPress, you can easily link your site to the other bloggers' sites, and everyone can benefit from the mutual exchange. Before you know it, friends of friends bookmark your blog (or simply click their way to it through mutual friends) and you have a big party line.

Make no mistake; this is the secret to blog traffic, not simply writing great content. Do you ever notice how all the top blogs on the Internet (that is, quality writing blogs, not celebrity blogs!) are filled with comments? They are on top because they stimulate conversation among a devoted audience.

Article marketing

This is generally a good way to get targeted traffic to your website(S) someone has to actually read your article and then click on the link to visit your website .After reading your article , they will know what your site is all about ,make sure your info is attractive and this is the only way they can click your link.

You have to write an article based on the subject of your website and after submit it to article directories freely on: **knol.google.com, ehow.com, squidoo.com, ezinearticles.com, hubpages.com, articlebase.com, examiner.com, technorati.com, associatedcontent.com and buzzle.com.**

Make sure, the article must be keyword targeted just like your content this will enable people to find it.

You are meant to write 300 to 500 word articles based on your keywords.

Just a few years ago, article marketing was the all the rage. Linkbuilding (which is basically the process of building links across the Internet that lead back to your site) was of vital importance, and while links do matter, recent algorithm updates have changed the way links are counted, particularly 'low quality links'.

One of the easiest ways to identify low quality links, or so thought Google in May 2012, was to discriminate against the article directory website. It's easy to see why Google made that assumption, even though it might not be entirely fair. While there are some quality features on article directory sites, many other low quality pages can pollute the site and bring the search rankings down.

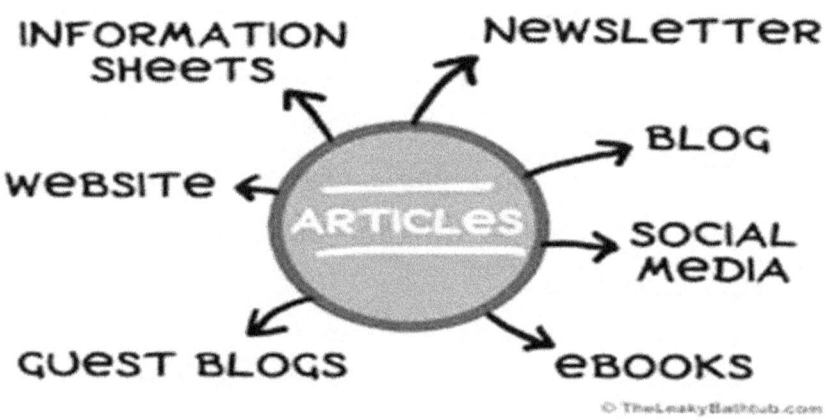

Article directories claim to have an editorial process, and truth be told, you can still find some top rated SERPs from article directory pages. However, experts within SEO have noticed a trend of article directory penalization. So, the safest thing to do is to diversify your linking strategy, perhaps investing a little bit in article directory marketing, as well as blogs, guest blogs, and press releases.

Press releases

A press release is a written statement to media. They can announce range of news items including scheduled events personal promotions, awards , new products and services , sales accomplishments etc. they can also be used in generating a feature story . Reporters are more likely to consider a story idea if they first receive a press release. it is a fundamental tool of PR work one that anyone who's willing to use the proper format can use , well you know to Write a genuine headline which should belief, clear and to the point , an ultra compact version of the press releases key point . plenty PR professionals recommend writing your headline at the end, after the end of the release is written. If you follow that instruction, continue on and come back to writing the headline.

Once the rest is done, the headline is known as the eye catcher and very important of the whole release.

You can browse this link: **www.wikihow.com/write-a-press-Release** and see samples of some pressmissing releases , this will help you more on how to write a proper press release and using keywords early will give you better visibility in search engines.

FAZE 3

Social marketing strategies

We all know that when you join these social networks ,you definitely need to market to users ,but first of all you need to put in mind that keep a social aspect lnfact .you need to talk to people ,chat with them and be friendly.

If you fail to keep this in your mind, people may not respond to your offers they will instead ignore you .first forget about selling on social networks, make friendship for at 80% and 20% marketing.

Viral facebook fan pages

Do you know what facebook fan pages are?_Facebook is a social networking site with over 600 million users, it has setup system where you can add a page to their site. This page could be a site for your online business, for you as a person, for a charity or cause or any thing else you would want.

By creating a fan page like this, you can then invite different people to like or join your fan page. These people will also invite all their facebook friends to also join your people that like your page, the more liked your page. This will make your page to go viral which means that it will keep getting massive amount of fans without you having to invite anyone.

The basic steps of setting up your facebook page are:

- Browse **https://www.facebook.com/pages/create/** to create your page.

- Select a category and Page name for your business

- Select a logo or image which can be associated with your business and use it as your profile picture.

- Let people know about your business and what you do by writing a sentence about it.

- Create a web address for your page that is memorable and can be used on your marketing material. This will help you promote your Facebook presence.

- The first thing people will see when they go to your Facebook page is your cover photo. Select one or create one that best represents your business.

Once you've developed your page, you can reach out to not only your current customers but also to other users on Facebook. You want to keep your posts as high quality and post regularly.

WHAT YOU SHOULD KNOW ABOUT: facebook

YOUR CUSTOMERS ARE ON FACEBOOK

more than **500 MILLION** active users

of which **50%** log on to Facebook every day!

spending over **700 BILLION** minutes per month

What used to be a place for college students and younger is now a place for everyone. According to new reports the fastest growing demographic on Facebook in 2010 is adults aged 55 and over. The largest overall demographic on Facebook is ages 35-54, which makes up 29% of all Facebook users.

54.8% of Facebook users are between the ages of **25 TO 54**

Facebook's Features

Facebook is a website that capitalizes on personal user relationships. Facebook is the place that boldly brings together friends, family members and acquaintances from all walks of life. In fact, many people actually avoid talking or even listing their business and instead just enjoy time off with their friends. We can blame a series of well-publicized Facebook 'Fails' for this, you know the boss is always watching when you make fun of the company in a public forum. So yeah, that and the fact that no one wants to swear in front of grandma, just keeps Facebook a very work-less environment. The moment you start mentioning work, people become annoyed. (Unless of course, you're complaining about work!) On the other hand, no one really cares what you say on your profile, because it's perfectly fine to say who you are, what you do and where you work. It's the sort of conversation you would have at a bar, right? Besides, people do actually want to know who you are, they want to know of what "use" you are to them. For example, if you say you're a doctor, everyone will definitely take note of that and call you up the next time they have a question. It's the same principle with anything you do, as soon as you say that you work in a certain field, you are deemed the expert and your associates identify you with your products and your business. No, they don't want to talk about it. They don't want to hear you rattle off catchphrases and talk about great deals. However, if an issue comes up they will definitely click your profile and visit your website. They will be seeking you out, looking help with their customer needs.

This is the secret to social networking, and quite frankly, the secret to all sales in the new millennium. Do not try to sell on Facebook, attract your customers. Besides the ability to create a detailed profile full of links, Facebook also has these other advantages:

- The Ability to Share Photos and Videos: Facebook allows you to share photos and videos among friends, which can be funny, touching, motivational or controversial. These are great at stirring reaction, and the more people you have chatting, the more your brand is getting around. After all, your goal is to be the brand. So, not talking about business is not really a big deal if you are using your personal time to promote your company's values.

- The Ability to Connect with New People: Facebook lets you connect with old friends (who it actually seeks out according to your personal Internet logs… creepy, huh?), reply to messages and send private messages. It also has various forms of communication, from direct conversation to status updates, to highlighting articles you have read, which others might be interested in. The point is, you can engage your audience on a social page and earn their respect as a friend, long before you ever bring up business. Creating a long list of contacts is the first step to using social networking, as you are building a large and personally invested audience. Remember to make your page public if you hope to get extra publicity. You can also like or share pages that are not only interesting to you, but reflect the values of your company.

In essence, your behavior is part of your brand. Out of curiosity, people will 'stalk' you just to see what you like, what you say and what you believe. It's all great for publicity!

Facebook Groups and Pages: Another example of Facebook's unique environment is the fact that you can create your own groups and pages and unite people (and secretly build an audience) to promote something you believe in. Now, you cannot convince them all to 'join' your company. True, you can ask people to "like" your company and bribe them to do so as well, but it's not as effective as drawing their attention away from business and towards a free group or fan page. Instead of trying to break down their resistance, distract them from business talk by focusing on another common agenda. Like a group of people united by a common interest, or a group of people who gather together locally to discuss issues. Creating a community away from business can actually draw people to your business, as they will soon realize you're a natural born leader and know a great deal about your industry (and how it affects them). Start by searching for existing groups and taking part in that discussion. The great thing about Facebook is that you never have to sign up to new groups. You simply use the same ID and can converse freely in a variety of connected 'worlds'. If your niche interest (which is also your business) doesn't exist, be sure to create it.

You can also create movie pages, celebrity pages and product pages just to get attention from the mainstream world, all of which may take an interest in your life and career. Be sure to research the keywords and determine what your group name should be called in order to drive more traffic to you. Keyword research tools or even Facebook searching tools can be of help here.

Facebook Places: See Faze 6 under Mobile and Local Free Advertising.

Facebook Events: Users can create events and gatherings and invite all of their friends to join them. Even if all the VIPs cannot RSVP, they can still comment on the event and offer moral support. Little events (whether a night out at dinner or a huge festival in town) sponsored by your company are a great way to get a dialogue going with others, or even to brand your name as an official sponsor of a "meet up" in person. For even better traffic generation, provide the details of your involvement at your official website.

About Twitter

Twitter in nutshell is a simple social networking website which lets you share with your friends known what you are doing right now. Therefore the old catch phrase on the twitter signup page." What are you doing?".

Think of facebook , instant messaging and sms all rolled into one simple package and you have got twitter.'

Twitter works around a timeline which is displayed on a single page which is update every second of every minute of every hour, I hope you get my point. It constantly updated stream of news from people all around the world. If you are a member, you can add your own little message to the timeline up to 140 characters long to it known as a tweet.

Linkedin

Linkedin is a professional network that has over 150 million members world-wide, it's the world's largest and most popular professional or equivalent of facebook for the professional world. If you don't know Linkedin, you better head over and create a profile, it makes sence to make it part of your social media plan. The plat-form is predicted to grow massively and play an important role in marketing activities of companies. Over 150 million Linkedin users world wide, atleast 2 new members sign up every second.

- In the UK there are more than 11 million Linkedin users

- Geneder ratio, 55% female and 45 % male

- Over 2.6 million companies have linkedin company pages.

- 69 of the top 100 fortune companies use Linkedin

- 50% of the top 100 fortune companies hire through Linkedin.

- 90% of Linkedin users think the site is useful because it helps them to connect with people from the respective industry as possible clients.

- There are over 10 million endorsements provided everyday

Here is how you get started with Linkedin:

1. **Personal Account**—The first thing you need to do is create a personal account on LinkedIn. To make a company account, you have to also have a personal one. To begin, just go to http://www.linkedin.com and enter the basic information. When you complete it, just click "Create My Profile."

2. **LinkedIn Profile**—Before you complete your profile,

a confirmation email will be sent to your email account. It will have a link in it you need to confirm your account. It will take you to the sign-in page where you enter your email and password.

3. **Linked in offers two services**—a basic "free" one and a premium "paid" one. After you choose the type you want, you'll be ready to click "Profile" and begin to edit your profile.

Create both your personal and company profiles.

For your LinkedIn profiles, it is recommended that you add a lot of information. All the information you enter is searchable, so the more you have, the better it is for your business, and the easier it is to be found. When you're finish preparing them, you can link your personal to your company profile. Add a detailed description of your business.

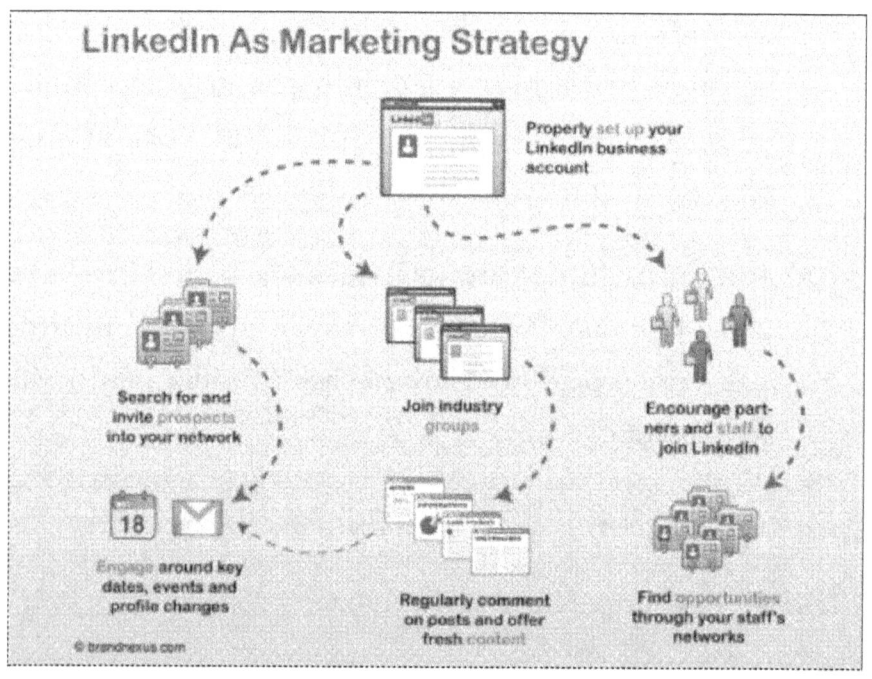

4. **Company website**—You'll see a field for your company's site and the type of industry. When you put your site, use the format: http://mywebsite.com. This will automatically become a hyperlink to your company from your personal profile. All the members of your staff can use this hyperlink to link back to your company. It's a great way to be seen. Your industry field is searchable, so think before you choose. It will be a very good way to find potential clients and for them to interact with you.

5. Get involved. LinkedIn is the same as any social media site. If you want to be seen, you have to get involved. Make connections and contacts to start building your network. The exposure will help lead you to a bigger audience. After you get set up on LinkedIn, there are several features that it has that can be useful to help build your business.

Here are a few:

1. LinkedIn Search. Search for others in your industry and/or for potential customers. The more you connect the bigger audience you will have.

2. Ads. You can look at several of the ads for businesses in your industry. This will let you see how they use LinkedIn Ads for paid advertising.

3. Import your email contacts. On LinkedIn you can import your email contacts from your email applications. This way you can begin to add LinkedIn connections to your existing email accounts.

4. Post Updates. Like Facebook and Twitter, LinkedIn ha a status update field. You can begin a conversation or post a link to an article you've written.

5. LinkedIn Groups. Like Google+ circles, LinkedIn ha groups. They are members who share a common interest in a specific topic. They help you build a community. This is great for your brand.

6. Reply to Updates--You can see all updates posted to LinkedIn. Begin conversations yourself or reply to someone else's update. If you choose, you can elect to only see message from your connections or even set your own criteria.

7. Banners, You can add up to three custom banners to your company page for free. You can use them to:

   - Take customer testimonials, highlight them, and link them to your page.

   - Link to and promote an upcoming event or webinar.

   - Improve your target market by highlighting and linking to your blog posts.

   - Promote a video you've posted on your business

   - Let others know of the various social channels so they can reach you there.

8. Post company updates each day. Post updates during

the time of day you get the most traffic. For most, it's in the morning. You can try different times to see what works best with your audience.

9. Send messages to your target market. Linked in has a Sponsored Inmail feature that works like email. You don't need them on your email list. It just works from your LinkedIn. This isn't a free service, but it can be worth it.

Google +

May be you thought that google+ is just a social site, you're in for a big surprise ,what has been created is, put simply , phenomenol tool for human communication and in business but it takes you to experience it, embrace it and get it. google+ will give you everything you need to use it as an individual or for business .checkout this complete guide to Google+ circle management:**www.martinshervington.com/what-is-google-plus.**

Here are a few ways you can use Google+ for your business:

1. Use the "About" section. This section gives you a chance to write a little about your business. Tell people what products/services you have to offer and what your business is all about. Google will use the introduction portion of this section in search results

2. Link other accounts. You can add links for your other social media profiles like Facebook, Twitter and LinkedIn. This is a good way to gain authority.

3. Circles. You can create circles on your Google+ account. For each circle, you want to add people based on your interests. Usually, if you add people to your circle, they will follow back. This way, when you start sharing your content, you increase the chances of exposure.

4. Share content with others. Here you can share your content with the world. In addition, you can share the content of others that you like. By sharing, you get your context indexed, no matter what you share.

5. Engage with others. Sharing is great, but if you want to move it up a notch, it's great to comment on what others are sharing. You can leave a comment or +1 what they've shared. It will make people want to add you to their circle. This, in turn, increases your chances of having your content shared.

6. Employee Google+ accounts. You can have your employees make their own profiles. That way, they can take a few minutes a day to post to your site, share your posts, or maybe even +1 your business.

If your business doesn't have a Google+ account, you will find definite search and social advantages to having one for your company.

Pinterest

Printerest is a pin-board style photo sharing website that allows users to create and manage theme based image collections such as events, interests and hobbies, users can browse other pin board for images " repin Images? To their own pin boards or like photos.

Forums

Many online marketing forums and internet business forums are full of very nice people that have a culture of helping each other out , this some times can be seen in some people offering free software and advise to other people on the forums , below are the compelling reasons why you should be participating in forums when promoting any internet business.

<u>Trust</u>: we work best with people we can trust and we promote and run internet business , joint ventures with

people we can trust , people who help others a lot also get help in return , the greater the degree of trust people have in you, the easier it is for you to make sales online.

The other reasons as to why people join forums is to carry out joint ventures , you will find there are so many success business people in forums with huge marketing email lists which they contact from time to time and they are looking for good products to recommend to their members, if you have a good product that you are selling and if you have a good relations with these big business owners , you can always be mentioned and their large subscribers lists, therefore you could make some good money in a such deal, therefore trust and friendship developed online can change into internet business money.

Back links

The majority of forums allow people to add lists to their signatures , the more links to your internet business website that you are looking at, the better for you in terms of visitors and search and engine visits as well . Always use the anchor text that you are interested in when adding a link to your signature in any website forum.

The more links which suitable anchor text pointing to you

website, the better your search engine rankings will be period.

Another point about the web forums is concerning people who love spam the forums, meaning that they put advertisements in places they should not. This is usually against the terms of use of forum, what happens is that the person can be warned and then banned always contribute nicely to the thread and then if you think your product solves a problem, point to your signatures nicely in your thread.

Publicity

The result publicity for any new service or product in large forums cannot be understated. Since there are so many large business owners in those forums, what happens is that once you have a new product that is good or popular and if you offer an affiliate program, you will be able to receive good publicity for any product that you are promoting in any internet business. This is a snow ball effect because people on one forum are usually in several forums and sometimes a new product can be discussed in many forums at the same time, imagine how much a publicity storm could kick up on your internet business profits.

Ultimately, when you participate in internet marketing

forums and helping other people along with good thing, you gain valuable back links from the search engine which boosts your search engine rankings, valuable publicity and most important , you gain trust which is a key in internet marketing community, spend time , cultivating your contacts in internet marketing forums and see such online networking reap huge dividends later.

FAZE 4

Email marketing

Let me hope that you are probably aware that email marking is the most powerful form of online marketing today. All top marketers use email to deliver their messages for one good reason. However, the huge proliferation of SPAM ever since the Internet first launched in the public eye has destroyed the reputation of legitimate email marketing. (SPAM is essentially, cold-emailing people with a business proposal…and especially with hyperbolic text promising the world). SPAM is also associated with overseas scam operations. Luckily, most of us are too smart to respond to these sneaky emails. Now if you can look past the SPAM approach, and convince your audience that you are not one of them, you will be able to generate traffic. The hard part comes in establishing a stellar reputation.

The difference between email marketing and spam

As you know, the internet is one of the most effective ways to market a new product or service especially for start-up businesses. However businesses need to be very careful how they go about trying to attract customers via the world of instant emails, as there is very fine line between sending out an email a customer has opted in for and the one that they have not this can be called SPAM.

An opt in email is any piece of commercial communication sent via email that the customer signed up to receive it can be a newsletter , free information , monthly sales brochure or any other type of correspondence from the company before .

opt in correspondence is initiated, the customer must give business their permission (sometimes twice) to send them emails before they can legally do so.

What is SPAM:

Spam is any type of commercial communication sent via email that the receiver has not given their permission to receive. normally emails which are personal do not fall under spam category unless you are sending multiple emails to your friends when you are promoting your product then they can be victimized as SPAM.

Benefits of opt in Emails:

The primary benefit of opt in emails is that you are building a custom list of customers who already have interest in whatever you have to offer .it will allow you to target your email marketing campaigns more correct , because your customers made a choice to receive communication from your company , you will definitely be protected should any of them report your emails as spam in future because you have an information proof that they gave permission to receive emails from your company.

More benefits of opt-in email campaign include:

It preserves your business one line reputation.

It will show your customers that you respect their privacy.

It will help you to create a long lasting relationships with your customers.

It will save you from having to buy lists which may not include your target audience.

It can increase product sales, profits and interests.

The disadvantages of spam.

All customers don't like to receive emails from businesses they are not interested in. emails will flood their inboxes and this will waste their a lot of time sorting them in order to get emails they want to read. Incase if you do not have your customers opt-in to receive in emails, you will definitely be sending spam after all its slightly less targeted means of direct mail marketing.It is along time tactic used by local companies, but the difference is it is online.

When many people tag your emails as SPAM, you are more likely to find yourself in trouble with (ISP) internet service providers, your email and ip address may end up being black listed, this will damage you online reputation and it will have a direct impact on your company success and you will find that all the money you spend creating and sending out emails will be wasted for nothing.

How to prevent your company increase your sales potential through opt-in emails.

If you want to effectively start marketing you online business through email wave, you have to do it correctly and have an opt-in form on your website. if you are seriously about marketing your business in a respectful and professional way, then include a sign-up form on your website and after the transaction is done successfully provide the customer with the opportunity to join your email list . your customers will appreciate the respect you offered to them then you will be able to put much attention on your marketing efforts to those who want your products and services the most.

How to create a mailing list

One of the most crucial ways of communicating with and building up your customer base is by creating a mailing list .

it's getting harder and harder to do that with new spam laws. Mail filters and the general consensus that signing up for a mailing list on a website will guarantee an instant quality of unwanted email.

Let us begin with how to build your list:

I advice that before you begin, you will need to start by creating a privacy policy you can find a free privacy policy generator by visiting the link below:

http://www.the-dma.org/privacy/creating-shtml

The above website will walk you through the steps of creating a rock solid policy that will enable your business to function smoothly and build customer confidence.

When you are done with creating your policy, you will need to post links on your website that are easily visible to your customers, it also a good idea to include a link to this policy on your page where you will be collecting your customers data.

The next step will be to figure how you would like to collect the customer data. There are quite many free mailing list managers available. you can choose between remotely hosted mailing lists which handles all the details for you, including a setup, storing information and sending out emails, before picking up a company to handle your remotely hosted list. You will need to make sure that they do not sell customer data and that they have a good reputation.

You might want to choose to install a software on your website which will create and manage your list, these programs often include a web include a web based control panel which simplifies to send out messages to your customers and maintain their data.

If your plan is to have a big list, make sure that your software has a capability of handling it , avoid the embarrassment of loosing data . Switchovers and the need to start from scratch. Incase you are planning to run the list manually using your email program to send out customer messages then make a frequent data back up.

Check with your webhosting service to see if the y require customers to double opt-in to your emailing list , basically this means that the customer will have to reply to an email generated by the list managing program before they are added to your list . this ensures that customers will not be included to lists that they have no desire be on and will help you to stand out from spammers.

If you are done with your technical issues, you can go to your business of building your list , make sure that customers can find your mailing list therefore you will need to post links on your website which are easy to find. It helps in the beginning stage to offer a free gift or free information as a motivation for customers to sign up . you can as well include a link to signup customers automatically if they place an order on your website.

Several sites now have pop-up windows to encourage signups and this increases your customers base importantly, however there is nothing more annoying than a persistent pop-up , it is best to have the popup appear once during a customer's session.

You have now got your customer list up running, how do you keep them interested and most importantly, how do you keep them coming back to your site for more? There is one simple way to do this and this is to offer a free ezine to your mailing list , this can keep them informed and increase their level of trust in you as a business , people feel more secure and confident when ordering products from companies they know . you may send out ezines daily, weekly ,or monthly as you may wish, make sure your customers know how often the ezine will be sent out a head of time to cut down on spam complaints.It is possible to run a profitable and an informative ezine in just a few minutes, proper planning and effective list management software will ensure your success in creating your own mailing list.

Autoresponders

Autoresponders are email utility that automatically replies to an email message with a pre-written response when that email comes into a specific email or internet address. Auto responders are used by individual and also by websites that needs to respond to user comments automatically for example :an individual may use an auto responder feature of email to inform the sender that he has gone on vacation and will not be replying personally to emails until he returns to the office, an enterprise may use an auto responder in response to a newsletter subscription request to verify the opt in or subscription cancellation or to indicate to the sender that a user comment was received. Auto responders are also used by enterprises to indicate that an online purchase was processed and will typically include and order confirmation number in the email that is automatically generated and sent to the purchaser

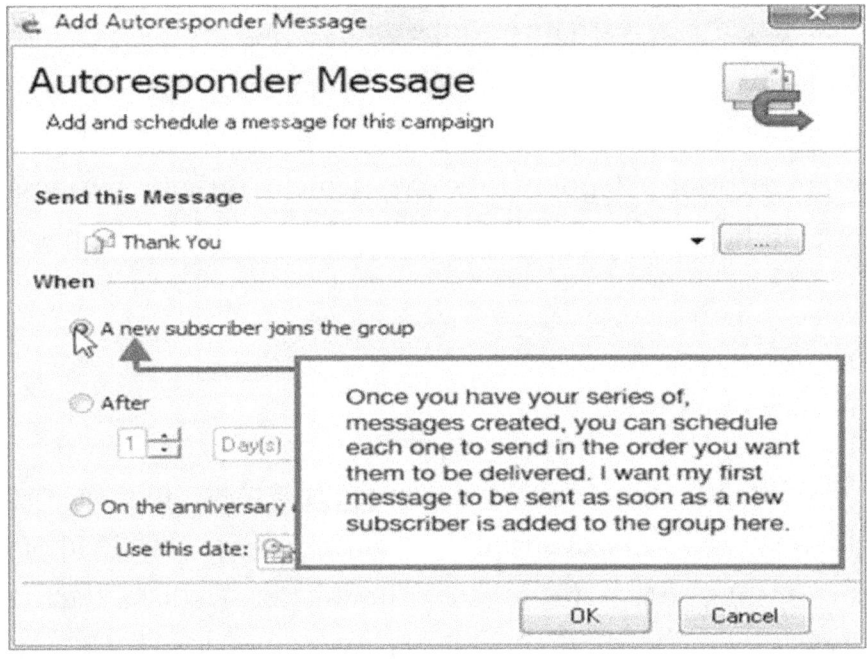

Autoresponder programmes

You can use programmes like: **www.aweber.com, www.getresponse.com**, and **www.rocketresponder.com**. The above auto responder programs will help you to send multiple email campaigns.

Newsletters

When you run a business, getting information out to your

stakeholders is extremely important to the success of the company. Your contacts include your employees, customers, shareholders and also your suppliers, in some cases. If you want to bring attention to some element of your business, one of the best ways is to use a newsletter.

What Is a Newsletter?

A newsletter is a short publication (normally one or two pages) that lists short articles of information, usually about an organization. A professional newsletter has an attractive template and clearly outlined sections for readers to browse. For instance, one article may contain general information about the company while another provides information about an employee of the month. Businesses use newsletters as marketing material, and they are sometimes integrated into a company's overall marketing plan. Companies print these publications, email them or publish them online for viewing.

The importance of newletter.

It allows the management to keep stakeholders informed about happenings at the company. An employee newsletter may contain information about new regulations or procedures that apply to the workforce. A newsletter to customers may provide information about a new technology the company uses or an article published in a major news outlet about the company. A newsletter also serves to remind people of upcoming events related to the firm.

It gives the company a format for notifying customers about new products and services. The company can print a picture of the product along with a detailed listing of its features and benefits. This is a simple and inexpensive way for a company to advertise when it releases new offerings. The newsletter also can display a special price discount for products or services advertised to encourage the reader to act and make a purchase immediately.

A company newsletter also serves as a branding tool. Branding is the process of establishing a unique look and focus for the company to make it more immediately recognizable to the public. A company can establish its brand by integrating its logo, motto and company colors into each newsletter. With a consistent branding theme, the reader may eventually start to look forward to the newsletter. Customers may recall and recognize all of the company's communications more readily in the future.

FAZE 5

Creating a Traffic Monster

Ultimately, you will never earn tons of traffic unless one of the two things come to pass: you get a huge following after years of creating an integrity customer base, or two, you go viral and get a small immediete fame fast. Well, when you build viral content on internet you can surprisingly get multiple sessions of 15 minutes. You can get exactly thousands of unique visitors within a few days, or may be even within a few hours if you hit it big. Just how does someone create viral content, the kind of content that creates a media impression and causes the snowball effect? The snowball effect is basically what happens when friends share content, and tell more people to do so, then finally everyone wants to view it because the world begins discussing it and it has happened numerous times before, whether we are talking about a cute baby video, a wonderful article, as well interview or even an urban legend that spreads all over the world.

Obviously, it's not all that easy to simply create something viral and hold on for the snowball effect to happen. Quite a number of pages have been created, sometimes according to the formula of viral content and with every objective of creating a storm of disagreement, but then they where disregarded. Its some how hard to predict what the Internet and what a million of friends of friends will find appealing and what they will think worthy of sharing. Bear in mind that no one feels compelled to share anything, just because the content is there. In order for someone to want to share interesting new content with other people, that person has to psychologically react to it.

considerably, it's sensible to say that people want to share unique content. Something that is new and hasn't been seen a hundred times before does sometimes get a big reaction. This is exactly why the majority of people choose to create video content hoping to brand their image.

Building Your Traffic Generation Strategy

In the next faze, we are going to discuss why Search Engine Optimization is the great technique for web advertising. This will be followed by a discussion of other online path. Long before you begin trying these techniques however, it is crucial to create aneffective traffic generation strategy. Consider it is a kind of mini-business plan, focusing exclusively on your internet marketing technique. Without a traffic generation plan, you will not really understand how effective your marketing is, nor will you be able to find a solution the ROI (Return On Investment) for all of your time spent. Your essential need here is to build a complete plan, then track your success, just as you would with an operational business system. Based on the results you notice, you will be able to decide your next course of action.

Truthfully, and as we are going to give a special importance in this book the best way to approach any marketing plan is to work on as many traffic generation methods as possibly can, rather than increasing efforts in one area, a plan that could very well rebound. Its better to put your eggs in different baskets. You want a complete web marketing plan that is going to initiate your website through multiple content development and link-building.

Eventually, the Internet is only a gathering of connected links. Within your website are a number of internal pages that allow observers and search robots to find all the pages accessible. When your site links to another site via an external link, more connections are made, making it easier for people to find you through this huge collection of links. It's fundamentally a computerized version of the whole "friend of a friend of a friend" dynamic. You definitely want your company, indeed, your brand, to be every where and all over the place, all over the Internet. This is exactly what huge websites like Amazon, Ebbay, Wal-Mart, Disney, Exxon-Mobile and many others. They expand themselves thick and they do it everywhere.

A Successful Traffic Generation plan.

- Develop a perfect step-by-step strategy, based on the information we are going to uncover in faze 2-6.

- Create a list of sensible goals, definite and based on your online progress, for instance. total number of links, PR rank, number one for targeted keywords, total traffic, sales conversions, leads, total sales, profit in sales, and many more.

- Create a means of tracking investment for time spent, any expenses you use, and make a comparison of profit / loss to decide if you are generating cash flow.

- Install analytics software on your site, either through individually pasting code into each page, or installing an application that analyzes your log files. Note trends and discuss these with your leadership team. Most web hosts offer site analytics for free, though Google also has its own

- When you are ready to begin the campaign, make sure you make changes to your website based on our upcoming recommendations and observe positive trends that you can benefit from.

Create the perfect you-tube marketing video and Audio

Did you know that you can use you-tube to market your business, product or service? However, you need a wonderful video in order to drive traffic and cause people want to visit your website after they have finished watching your Video. The majority of business sites don't have video and audio content, unless of course you're talking about corporate sites. Like recently ten years ago, small to pataining businesses usually never thought in terms of illustration presentation or practicle face-to-face sales. This is accurately why majoriy businesses are now creating video content online because of the idea that no body else is doing it. Well, that was the out-look when the big viral boom began first.

These days, a lot of small business are getting into the act and are producing their own practical videos, their own video presentations, and even their little comedy performance and short films. It all makes for better publicity. Even if you don't "go viral" and get millions of hits in a week, you may still make a lasting impression on your leads and that may very well convert these leads into paying customers. A lot of paying customers will make for a traffic increase. Audio presentations are also very big right these days, mostly if you plan on reaching targeted customers on for instance, PDAs, eBook players, Smartphones, multimedia players and many other. Some businesses have found great success in hosting a radio show or podcast, and talking about issues that are directly related to their business. Not only can an audio show or audio clips help to get better listening traffic on your site though you will possibly have to store content, but you can also direct the show's listeners back to your website to push merchandise.

The most essential things to remember when preparing video or audio content is, Keep it professional, practice dialogue and prepare the view with a director's eye, paying attention to details

 Its always very crucial to use only quality cameras to shoot video, Keep all videos and audio content appropriete to your business.

Do not hard advertise; simply replicate your own professional values in the content you give out. Make the content educational or interesting, not just video covering well known or " destructive" subjects. Look for "niches" that have not been done yet, you can also use a search engine to search for accessible videos of your idea. Create the most search-requested videos which don't exist yet and remember to tag your content with text also, or else your content might not be searchable at all. However, it may shock you to know that Google is already promoting new audio search technology that may greatly advance in the time to come.

Where to Host Your Content

This might be an easy step for you too, is that right? Not

essentially. Many people actually do want to host heavy video and audio content on their main site, they will definitely benefit from all the traffic if the content goes viral. On the other hand, this will take up vast amounts of web space and bandwidth (believe me, you don't actually have "unlimited bandwidth" and you may wind up having to select for a devoted server which will definitely cost you much money sooner or later, I want to let you know that some hosting companies don't allow video streaming on their shared servers simply because this can cause server overload, what you have to do is to install your embedded video links from you-tube, so you have to be careful.

Not surprisingly many business owners desire to work through a free storage site, or perhaps a social networking site that allows the storing of very large files. Some of the most clear sites for storage include YouTube, you can even build your own channel, links and store all of your videos in one position, Facebook , you can store videos on your own page) and a handful of other sites like DailyMotion, MetaCafe and etc. " For some reason even if, extra large Upload doesn't look to work anymore " Besides these two options, you have a third one: host your large content on a storage site and then just link to it with your social networking page or your official website. The great news is that a few cloud storage services (the biggest thing in online business today) are free. Cloud servers are a great idea, as they allow you to distantly back up your content so that data damage is never an issue anymore.Some servers even have auto update features, meaning you auto save new files on the cloud server just as soon as you save it to your hard drive, and the possibility for a user to access his / her content from anywhere and using any device. others even allow video replaying!

Free cloud servers include:

- DropBox (2 gigs free)

- SugarSync (5 gigs free)

- ZumoDrive (2 gigs free)

- Team Drive (2 gigs free)

- Ubuntu (2 gigs free)

- iDrive (5 gigs free)

- OpenDrive (5 gigs free)

- Syncplicity (2 gigs free)

- SpiderOak (2 gigs free)

- SkyDrive (2 gigs free)

- Google Drive (5 gigs free)

The importance of pictures

Majority of people think the page rank (pr) is about press release, text and words which to a certain extent it is however, the importance of images cannot be under rated.Pick-up a magazine or a newspaper near you and have a flip through, I strongly believe that good stories with additional image are the ones that get your attention for that case good images are essential when trying to achieve press coverage.

I realized that one of the biggest problems we face is people who do not understand the importance of images, so below are some guidelines on images and how and why you should use them.

1. A picture says thousand words-whether its product image, an image of you and your team or images from an event , including an image in your press release will grab a journalist's attention and help you tell you

story.

2. You might need different images, its important to have a variety of shots, from your product in action, to cut outs to your product on a plain white back ground, in that way you shots will be appropriate for most uses.

3. Its always a good idea to invest in a proper photo shoot, never under estimate what a photographer can do for your brand, outside of the business of actually taking the photos , a good photographer can advise on the kind of images you need to show your business to its best advantage , provide lighting and professional back drops and develop creative ideas to really make you stand out from the crowd.

4. Avoid amateur photo shooting –if you cant avoid a proper shoot, its best to avoid making the shots up ,badly photo shopped images are obvious and wont do you brand any favours.

5. Finally the most importantly , news proper and magazines can only use high-res images , so its essential that any images you send have a resolution of over 300 dpi (dots per inch) and are atleast 1MB.

Social book marking

This is a way for people to store, organize, search and manage "bookmark" of web pages. So that other people can publicly see incase If you bookmark useful content other people will find it, share it, vote it up for other people to enjoy it.

Below are the top five social book marking sites:

1. Twitter : with over 200 million people
2. Delicious: with over 5 million people
3. Digg: with over 26 million people
4. Reddit: with over 17 million people
5. Stumble upon: with over 17.5 million people

Make sure you visit all the above sites, look at them well and learn how they operate.

FAZE 6

Banner advertisement

Banner advertisement is a rectangular graphic display that stretches across the top or bottom of a website or down the right or left sidebar. The former type of banner advertisement is called leader board , while the latter is called a skyscraper. Banner ads are image based rather than text-based and area popular form of website advertisement.

The purpose of banner advertisement is to promote a brand and /or to get visitors from the host website to go to the advertiser's website.

The host is paid for the banner advertisement through one of the three methods: cost per impression (payment for every website visitor who sees the Ad) cost per click(payment for every website visitor who clicks on the ad and visits the advertiser's website), or cost per action (payment for every website visitor who clicks on the ad goes to the advertiser's website and completes a task such as filling out a form or making a purchase).

Keep banners simple and make sure you convey a message...not merely an attitude or a thought that leads nowhere.

There are "standards" of banner sizes to regard. Below are standard sizes to choose from:

468 x 60   Full Banner

728 x 90   Leaderboard

336 x 280   Square

300 x 250   Square

250 x 250   Square

160 x 600   Skyscraper

120 x 600   Skyscraper

120 x 240   Small Skyscraper

240 x 400   Fat Skyscraper

234 x 60   Half Banner

180 x 150   Rectangle

125 x 125   Square Button

120 x 90   Button

120 x 60   Button

88 x 31   Button

Nevertheless, to trading banners with other companies, networks or search directories, you can also set up banners for affiliate network opportunities or even for self promotion. So yes, it is a smart idea to create a banner now before you suddenly find out that you need one and have nothing in the word

Pay Per Click (PPC) Advertisement

Pray per click (PPC) is an internet advertising model used to diver traffic to websites in which advertisers pay the publisher (a website owner), when the ad is clicked. However PPC is not always associated with free website traffic generation.The most popular pay per click advertisement networks are (google adwords, facebook, yahoo, search marketing and Microsoft ad center Bing.

Free ppc Advertising credits:

Most of ppc advertising networks like (google adwords , yahoo search marketing , Microsoft Ad center , Ask.com Bid advertises miva etc) offer free Ad credits to attract customers. Another popular site with free ppc is squidoo lenses, squidoo is a very popular place to easily make small web pages and they are called lenses **http://www.squidoo.com** . A lens is simply a page regarding a specific topic that you choose to write about , if you lens is live , it can be found by other people when they search for keywords related to your lens.

You are free to make as many lenses as you want , so if you want to make about 50 lenses , you can go ahead you can also make money off of your lenses, you can get paid from clicking on Amazon ads , Ebay ads and google ads on your lens , there is a maximum & 10 payout . you can choose to be paid in all cash to donate any revenue you make to a charity or a 50/50 combination of both.

Affiliate programs and Joint venture campaigns

It is very simple to get affiliates for your program if you announce or declare that you will provide attractive commission for their sales and run a good joint venture campaign, then you can see that hundreds of people joining your affiliate, its almost very simple to get affiliate for your program. Affiliate program usually acts as intermediary between affiliates and retailers who are in need of selling their products. It's up to to choose to be either an affiliate or a retailer you need to first of all read and understand the terms and conditions of the affiliate program of your choice and abide with them.

If you're an affiliate, pick up a product of your choice that you are willing to promote and checkout for some favourite banner sizes, text ads and some other options.

Why affiliate marketing?

- No expensive start-up costs.
- No stocks to hold or orders to fullfil.
- You only need a computer and internet connection.
- There is No limit to the amount you can earn.

I want to let you know that even the top affiliates today where once complete beginners.

Sellers: if you're using an affiliate program to back up your sells, please know that it's not easy to keep affiliates to continue working for you.

The main reason as to why people join your affiliate is to earn money, so if your competitors provide higher affiliates commission for selling a similar product, then your affiliate will definitely stop working for your competitor's product.

Provide good training and support for your affiliates, they will only work for you if they get some good profit for promoting your product.

Ask yourself, how will they promote if they have no knowledge about your product? This may result in poor performance of the affiliate and finally they will certainly lose interest in your product. Always provide your affiliate with good training and support whenever they need it, you should also provide them with all details about your product as well as some promotional tools and tips such as logo, product pictures and banner explaining the product, and this will make life of your affiliate easy and they will enjoy working with you.

Lastly, provide your affiliates with multiple payment options which are famous or supported in different parts of the world.

Giving away free stuff

Its always good to give away free stuff in order to generate lots traffic to your website , this could in exchange to their visit, you can offer donated goods, monthly contents .if your giving away something which is wonderfully amazing , this will boost the popularity of your website traffic .

Website visitors love contents and many of them are willing to visit the same sites each day just to enter to win something free. Therefore by offering free stuff through a contest, you are likely to get visitors to return on a daily basis . Set the rules to state that each visitor can only enter once a day you like. Purchase a good prize or get one donated and give it away to the random name drawn from the entries , this is a great way to get the attention of many consumers, especially if your prizes are very interesting and worthy .

If you really want to spread the word on your website and get more traffic than ever, you should consider giving referral prizes you can set your system up in order to allow each visitor to send and automated email from your site as them to visit, if the visitor is willing to offer up to 10 or 20 valid email addresses, them you can offer them a free prize . the prize can be as small or large as you would wish. This is a great way to generate more traffic while also rewarding those that are helping you along the way.

Mobile and Local free Advertising

Here are come to some other big thing in traffic, as a matter of fact both smart phones and tablets have really become an integral part of our lives and as a result, consumers expect a seamless digital experience regardless of device they are using.

Did you know that 120 million people in US own smart phones and 48 million people own tablets, the tablet is the fastest growing electronic device currently. These devices are used mostly for texting, using social media and telephoning as well as email/im place fourth.

36% of people in US purchase goods or products online using their mobile marketing focuses on mobile device users especially for those who travel a lot will create text messages for marketing especially for social networks.

You've got to look for your audience whenever they move to and even if they go mobile for marketers mobile is just another way of reaching their target audience and the objectives is sales. Below are leading objectives for mobile marketing according to business executives' world wide.

59% - increase sales

52% -improve customer service/convenience.

49% -increase brand awareness

45% -Acquire new customers

14% -Grow mobile opt in list

13% -Grow email opt in list

6% -Lower support costs

5% -Don't know

You could also consider the new technology of local marketing and this is possibly made through mobile devices which can assign all of your internet information.

Consider the biggest local sites for your mobile marketing campaign such as : Google places , google maps and facebook places.

 When you sign up at all the above sites its an added advantage for you to reach the attention of people within your local vicinity facebook places and google places are one of the biggest search engine giants for local business and they can as well send mobile traffic to your company basing on where you and your customers are located.

Google maps can help your business to grow as it can be a major player in the online marketing campaign forefront. In today's scenario if people get lost, the first thing they should do is to log into google maps and check for directions. Google maps can as well send local website traffic via devices to your company.

Take your marketing offline

It is very obvious that there is still many people out there who do not get all of their information online. Some of the people use the internet for business or email and they occasionally purchase online. Therefore if you want to reach them, you have to do it offline.

There are numerous ways to make people aware of you and your business , offline their income is not the same , some are better than others depending on your business but they all share common purpose with the online techniques . put your business name front of as many people as you can as often as you can , if many people get exposed to your message , many people will get to your site , more people at your site will mean more sales many companies have managed to the next level by many different things for people like printing T-shirts , making pans calendars and etc.

there company name s, logos ,and websites appear everywhere.

But for your case , you may atleast be able to make business cards and give them out to different people whom you may be able to talk to personally.

Tips and great ideas

I want to let you know that the internet is a great way to make money, but you actually have no ideal where to begin or what to do. Our step by step proven traffic methods will help both newbies { beginners } and those who have been online trying to find their success for some time, our methods makes it easy for any one to succeed online and you will quickly know what strategies to use in order to get results.

Always dream big, that's to be an interpreneur, believe it or not, some people luck confidence of being interpreneurs and yet its not a matter of intelligence either, there are many people who really want to work online but because they had no that interpreneur mind-set, they where unable to proceed.

They never even bothered about doing business, so as a result, they never made any money, so if your someone who thinks you can join online business on Sunday and get rich on Wednesday, you are not the kind of person that we want, you are a problem to me and every body else.

If you have a mind-set of getting rick quick, perhaps you can rob a bank or a forex bureau, we have nothing to do with that either. So you are the kind of person who is not emotionally stable enough to be an entrepreneur, then you're out. You simply don't qualify, you will be wasting your time and money, I advise you to continue to stay at your current daily job or wait until the right job comes.

Are you selling other people's products? Yes its possible to earn a living that way, but such successes are rare.

Create your own product: then you can use affiliate programs to back-end sales, you will control your destiny, you will control how it is marketed, you will control how much profits you make.If you would like to hire people to do for you various aspects of your marketing : like making videos writing articles ,press releases ,creating blogs and etc it's for aslow as 5$ and you can find people to do this for you on any site of your choice below:

http://fiverr.com

http://forums.digitalpoint.com/form display.php?f=60

http://warriorforum.com

http://rentacoder.com

http://vwriter.com

Are you ready to live the internet life style?

If you have the enough courage persistence and desire to change your life, if you are the kind of person who dreams to be an entrepreneur and living life on your terms and freedom, adventure and true wealth { true financial security } for you and your family aswell, then A.T.S { Affordable Traffic Solutions } is the best for you.

Conclusion and a word of encouragement

We have really learnt quite a number of traffic generation methods in this e-book, keep in mind that building and growing a business requires research and careful planning.

It's up to you and how quickly you want to build your online business and this was created just for you and aspiring internet marketers like you people who actually DON'T want to waste time with cluttered path , people who want to build and grow online business which meets their needs ,dreams , expectations and goals of success.

Congratulations: you are now on your way to achieve your online dreams and expectations.

About the author

Lukwago Juma is a Ugandan, born and grew up in Kampala, Uganda having lost both of his biological parents who where already divorced while he was very young and where ugandans by descent aswell, he is the third child out of eight in his family. He studied from Kololo High school and unfortunately he couldnot afford to proceed to the university because of luck of finances to pay for his tuition, he begun his computer training, after words, he realised that there was money to be made on internet, so he begun as an affiliate promoting physical products and went through alot of training online and learnt numerous online marketing skills.

He learnt numerous proven traffic methods, eventually he wrote his first book called '' Affordable Traffic Solutions '' and he also wrote a book called '' challenges for an African child '' here you will read and know the challenges that an African child goes through in life, it's a story which he has gone through personally.

Otherwise. Today his personal achievements include , afilliate, online marketer, online coach and an author which has given him a lot freedom in his life and he is so thankful to God.

The author, Lukwago Juma can be contacted on: **jluke2008@gmail.com**, Tel: +256-752-538372, you can aswell checkout his below website: **www.jamesinfomedia.com**

www.ingramcontent.com/pod-product-compliance
Lightning Source LLC
Chambersburg PA
CBHW071751170526
45167CB00003B/997